W9-ACV-794

NATURE'S CHILDREN™

LICE

by Katie Marsico

Children's Press®

An Imprint of Scholastic Inc.

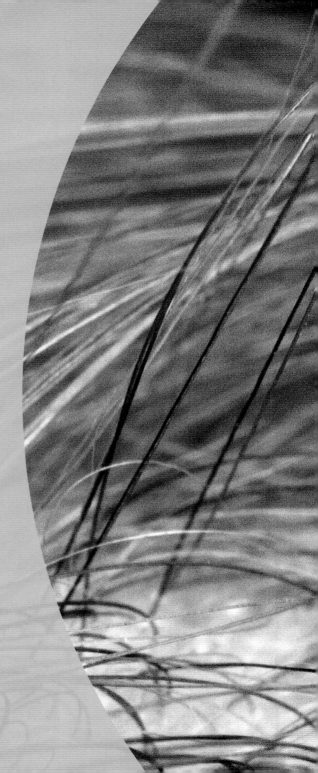

Content Consultant
Dr. Stephen S. Ditchkoff
Professor of Wildlife Sciences
Auburn University
Auburn, Alabama

Photographs ©: cover: David Scharf/Science Source; 1: Science Picture
Co/Superstock, Inc.; 2, 3 background: Hughhamilton/Dreamstime;
4, 5 background: Thailand Wildlife/Alamy Images; 5 top inset: Steve
Gschmeissner/Science Source; 5 bottom inset: omgimages/Thinkstock;
6, 7: Jean Paul Chassenet/Dreamstime; 8, 9: BSIP/UIG/Getty Images;
10, 11: Kallista Images/Superstock, Inc.; 12, 13: Biophoto Associates/
Science Source; 14, 15: Steve Gschmeissner/Science Source; 16,
17: Flirt/Superstock, Inc.; 19: Dennis Kunkel Microscopy, Inc./Visuals
Unlimited/Corbis Images; 20, 21: Steve Allen/Dreamstime; 23:
Science Picture Co/Superstock, Inc.; 24: Chassenet/BSIP/The Image
Works; 27: Wayne Hutchinson/age fotostock; 28, 29: Hughhamilton/
Dreamstime; 31: Centers of Disease Control/Superstock, Inc.; 32: Siri
Stafford/Getty Images; 35: Steve Gschmeissner/Science Source; 36,
37: Thailand Wildlife/Alamy Images; 39: beichh4046/Thinkstock;
40, 41: omgimages/Thinkstock; 44 background, 45 background:
Hughhamilton/Dreamstime; 46: Science Picture Co/Superstock, Inc.

Library of Congress Cataloging-in-Publication Data
Marsico, Katie, 1980– author.
  Lice / by Katie Marsico.
      pages cm. — (Nature's children)
  Summary: "This book details the life and habits of lice"— Provided
by publisher.
  Includes bibliographical references and index.
  ISBN 978-0-531-21395-7 (library binding)
— ISBN 978-0-531-21498-5 (pbk.)
1. Lice—Juvenile literature. I. Title. II. Series: Nature's children (New
York, N.Y.)
  RA641.L6M37 2016
  595.7'56—dc23   2014048014

Printed in China 62
SCHOLASTIC, CHILDREN'S PRESS, and associated logos are
trademarks and/or registered trademarks of Scholastic Inc.

1 2 3 4 5 6 7 8 9 10 R 25 24 23 22 21 20 19 18 17 16

Lice

Class	Insecta
Order	Phthiraptera
Families	Around 25 families
Genera	More than 200 genera
Species	Around 3,500 species
World distribution	Worldwide
Habitat	Near or on birds and mammals that serve as host organisms, with general preference for warm, moist areas
Distinctive physical characteristics	Bodies are shades of gray, white, tan, yellow, and bluish black; abdomen divided into 8 to 10 segments; antennae divided into three to five segments; flattened body and six thick, strong legs; clawlike feet; chewing species have broad, blunt head; sucking species have narrow, long head; small eyes or no eyes
Habits	Frequently remains with the same host organism throughout its entire life cycle; generally eats four to eight times a day and digests food quickly; females lay up to 10 eggs a day in warm, moist areas on host organism; moves by crawling; often coexists with other lice on the same host organism
Diet	Sucking species consume blood and other bodily fluids from various mammals; chewing species eat tiny skin, feather, hair, or fur particles from various birds and mammals

Contents

CHAPTER 1

The Source of an Itchy Scalp

A fourth-grader struggles to concentrate on his math test. He didn't get much sleep the previous night, so he is very tired. He kept waking up because his head itched terribly! He scratched so hard that he noticed sores on his scalp when he woke up in the morning.

Several hours into the day, the unlucky student doesn't feel much relief. To make matters worse, another unpleasant feeling has joined the itchiness. It's almost as if something is tickling his hair—or perhaps crawling through it!

The fourth-grader isn't going crazy. He has a bad case of head lice! Fortunately, he tells his parents about what he's experiencing. After identifying the cause of his discomfort, they use medicine to get rid of the lice. The itchiness goes away, and the boy can sleep soundly once again.

Head lice can cause itching and other unpleasant feelings on the scalp.

Where Lice Live

Lice are **parasites**. Parasites rely on other organisms for food or shelter while offering few or no benefits in return. Lice feed on **warm-blooded** animals such as birds and mammals. For certain **species** of lice, these host organisms serve as both a food source and a **habitat**. For example, human head lice spend the majority of their time on a person's scalp. These lice prefer warm, moist areas, including behind the ears and along the neckline. Unlike head lice, human body lice dwell in people's clothing and bed linens. They travel from these locations to feed on nearby human hosts.

Lice are generally found in the same environments as their host organisms. Because birds and mammals exist on every continent on Earth, so do the lice that feed on them. Most lice don't live long after losing access to a host organism. And, in many cases, they remain with the same host for their entire lives.

FUN FACT! Some lice make their homes in people's eyelashes and eyebrows.

Body lice, such as the one pictured here, are a different species than head lice.

An Overview of Appearance

Like most other insects, lice are quite small. Despite how much discomfort they sometimes cause, the majority of lice are tinier than a sesame seed. Most of the roughly 3,500 species measure between 0.04 and 0.16 inches (1 and 4 millimeters) long. It's not uncommon for females to be slightly larger than males. Lice can be many different colors, including gray, white, tan, yellow, and bluish black.

These wingless **invertebrates** have a flattened body and six thick, strong legs that end in clawlike feet. A louse's **abdomen** is divided into 8 to 10 segments. Lice that chew their food usually have a broad, blunt head. Species that suck blood or other bodily fluids have a narrower, longer front section.

Some lice have small eyes, while others have no eyes at all. Like almost all insects, they have a pair of feelers called antennae. Lice antennae tend to be short and are made up of three to five segments.

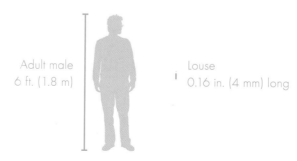

Adult male
6 ft. (1.8 m)

Louse
0.16 in. (4 mm) long

Lice can be very difficult to spot with the naked eye.

CHAPTER 2

Far from Fragile

Lice may be small, but they are tough survivors. Scientists believe they have existed on Earth for hundreds of millions of years. This is partially because lice face very few natural **predators**. In some cases, however, ants and certain monkeys have been known to eat them.

Humans pose a bigger threat to lice than other animals do. People have figured out how to use a variety of techniques to prevent and eliminate louse **infestations**. Yet in spite of human pest-control efforts, thousands of species of lice have managed to survive since prehistoric times. Along the way, they've developed many remarkable **adaptations**. They have also grown accustomed to feeding on many different hosts.

Chewing lice eat tiny skin, hair, feather, and fur particles. They attack hosts ranging from hawks and hummingbirds to guinea pigs and kangaroos. Meanwhile, sucking lice mostly feed on blood. They're attracted to hosts such as humans, squirrels, deer, seals, and elephants.

Despite their small size, lice can cause trouble for some of the largest animals on Earth.

Host-Specific Features

Different species of lice are often host specific. In other words, each type of louse is generally attracted to one particular type of host. For example, guinea pig lice don't normally chew on human skin or hair particles. Nor do human head lice usually obtain nourishment by sucking guinea pig blood. As host-specific parasites, certain lice have developed adaptations to support their unique feeding habits.

One example of this can be seen in louse species that attack seals, otters, and other marine mammals. All lice have breathing holes called spiracles in their skin. However, these slits have developed in the marine species in a way that helps them stay underwater for long periods.

A marine louse's abdominal area also features scalelike bristles called setae. While these stiff hairs are common in many invertebrates, they serve a special purpose in marine lice. The setae trap air, which makes it easier for a louse to breathe after its host organism submerges.

Some species of lice feed on hair, fur, or skin particles, while others feed on bodily fluids such as blood.

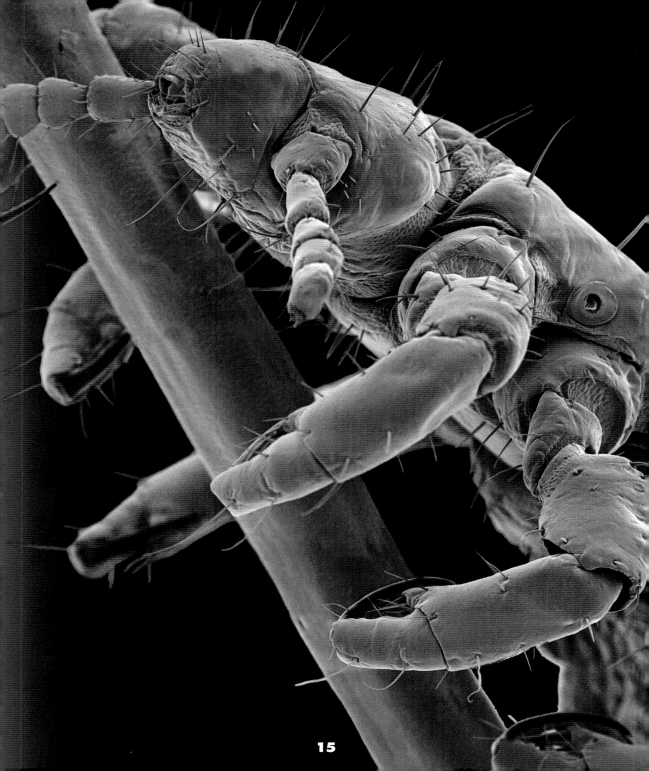

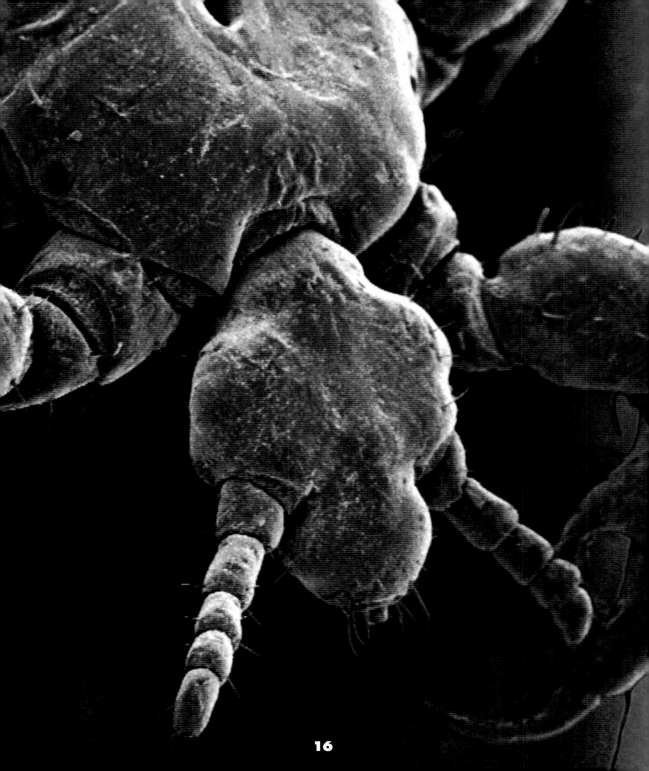

Crawling and Clutching

Lice must be able to move to locate food and mates. However, they are limited in their range of motion. Most don't jump or hop. Because they lack wings, they aren't able to fly either. Instead, these parasites often crawl to get wherever they need to go.

A louse's six powerful legs help it travel across—and remain attached to—various surfaces. At the end of some or all of its legs are one to two claws. A typical louse claw includes a larger curved segment and a smaller thumblike spine. This arrangement allows lice to firmly grasp on to a host's hair, feathers, or flesh.

Depending on the species, a louse's claws are sometimes different shapes and sizes. For instance, claws tend to be smaller in human head lice, which crawl through people's hair. These smaller claws make it easier for the lice to grab on to slender human hairs.

FUN FACT! Lice sometimes travel from one host to another by hitching a ride on larger, more mobile insects such as flies.

Up close, a louse claw looks much like a lobster claw.

Remarkable Mouthparts

Chewing and sucking louse species each have unique mouth features. Many chewing lice eat with a pair of mandibles, which are jaws used to scrape at and crush food. This is why chewing species have a broader head than sucking species. Their mandibles and jaw muscles take up more space.

Instead of mandibles, the majority of sucking lice have a tube-shaped sucking organ called a proboscis. The proboscis holds three sharp, rigid mouthparts called stylets. Stylets function like extremely sharp straws. A sucking louse relies on them to pierce a host organism's flesh. Then it drains blood up through its proboscis. When the louse is done feeding, it retracts its proboscis into its head.

Mandibles and stylets also serve as hooks. They allow lice to latch on tightly to host organisms. This prevents the parasites from falling off a host while they're eating.

The dog-chewing louse has mouthparts that help it feed on the skin and hair of dogs.

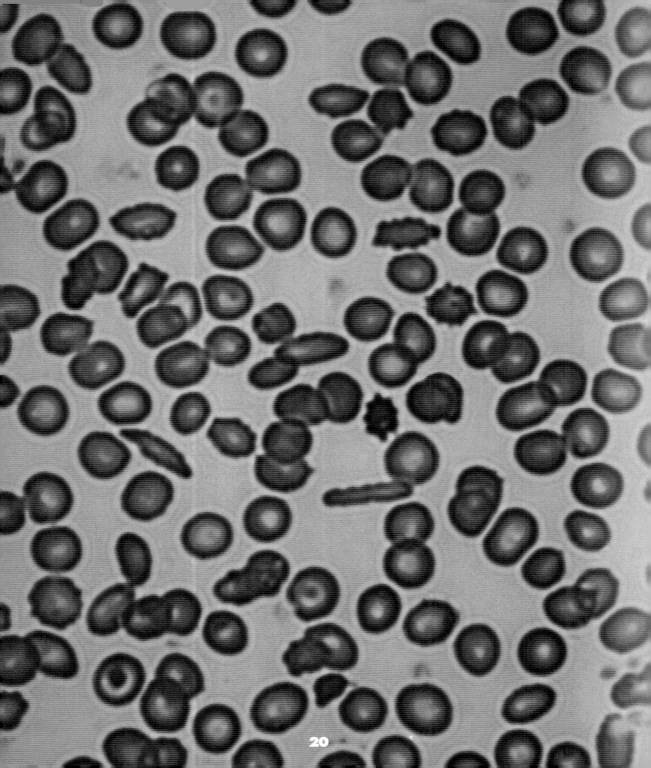

Highly Efficient Feeders

Saliva is another important feature within a louse's feeding process. It often contains chemicals that numb the areas where lice feed. As a result, host organisms don't immediately notice that they have been infested. This makes it easier for lice to eat without interruption.

Anticoagulants are present in the saliva of sucking lice. These chemicals stop the host's blood **cells** from clotting, or clumping together. As a result, blood flows more freely through the lice's stylets. Anticoagulants also prevent harmful blockages from forming inside lice that have just fed.

Lice generally eat four to eight times a day. They need to feed often because they digest food quickly. For certain sucking species, blood alone does not supply enough nutrition for their survival. Scientists believe that **bacteria** living in the digestive system of sucking lice provide the parasites with extra nourishment.

Blood cells clot together to prevent an animal from bleeding excessively when it is injured.

Sensory Skills

Although lice have weak vision and are not able to perceive clear images, some species are extremely sensitive to light. Many seem to prefer darker environments. If conditions suddenly become brighter, lice frequently respond by crawling away. For example, when a person's hair is parted, human head lice usually attempt to hide. This is why people don't always immediately observe parasites on their scalp.

Lice use several other adaptations to process information about their surroundings. They don't have ears, but they can probably detect vibrations with their setae. In addition, lice have sensory cells on their antennae and in their mouth. These cells help them taste and smell. It is even possible that species such as slender pigeon lice may identify and seek out hosts based on their odor.

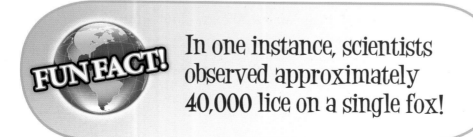

FUN FACT! In one instance, scientists observed approximately 40,000 lice on a single fox!

Antennae provide important sensory information that helps a louse navigate through its environment.

Shutting Down to Survive

Many lice can't survive more than a day or two without a host organism to provide nourishment. At most, some species are able to survive on their own for roughly a week. However, lice can be remarkably hard to kill when they have regular access to a host.

Efforts to end a louse infestation often include everything from **home remedies** to **pesticides**. Not all of these solutions are effective, let alone foolproof. This is because lice have a special ability that makes them extremely good at responding to threats.

Most remedies for lice infestations involve trying to drown, smother, or poison the insects. However, when these treatments are applied, lice can simply close their spiracles to keep out harmful substances. They also reduce activity within their nervous system. Some lice can survive this way for up to two hours while submerged in pesticide. In addition, scientists suspect that lice have developed a resistance to various chemical treatments. All of these combine to make lice a tough pest to be rid of.

Special shampoos and other treatments can help get rid of lice, but they are not always completely effective.

CHAPTER 3

A Louse's Life Cycle

Compared to the host organisms they feed on, lice don't usually live long. Depending on their access to a host, a louse's average life span is one to three months. They spend most of this time in close quarters with other lice. In cases of extremely bad infestation, tens of thousands of lice may coexist on the same host organism.

It is common to find more female than male lice living on a host. For every male human head louse present on a person's scalp, there are typically five females. In species such as cattle-chewing lice, only the females play a role in **reproduction**. Cattle-chewing lice are able to reproduce asexually. This means they do not need to mate with other lice to produce young. However, most species practice sexual reproduction, which requires both a male and a female partner. Adult lice often mate multiple times, but many females are capable of producing nits, or eggs, for the rest of their life cycle after mating just once.

Farmers often spray their cattle with special chemicals to help prevent infestations of cattle-chewing lice.

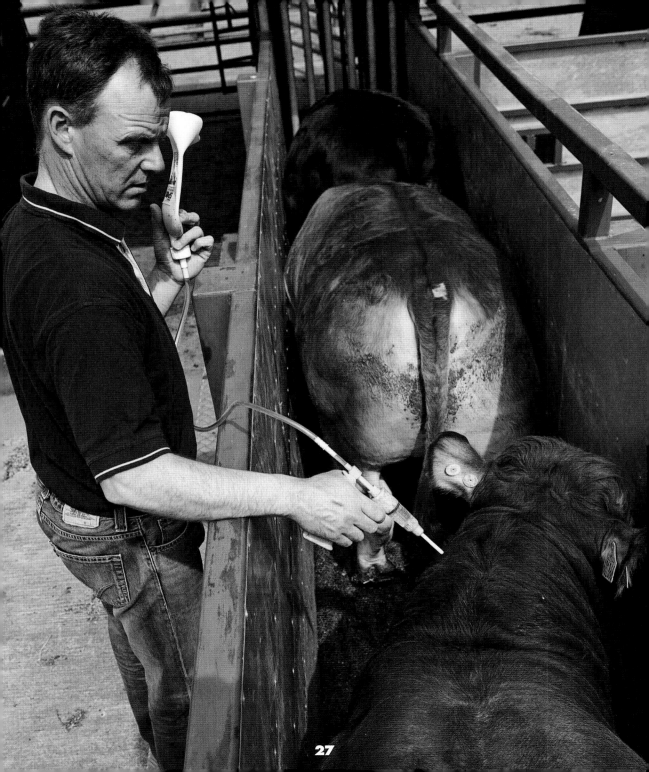

An Overview of Eggs

Once a female louse has mated, she can lay up to 10 nits a day. Females frequently place their eggs in warm, moist areas close to a host's skin. An exception to this rule occurs with human body lice. Their eggs tend to be found along the seams of clothing or bedding.

It is common for nits to serve as one of the earliest clues of a louse infestation. Unlike lice that have already hatched, nits can be easier to spot because they can't move to avoid detection. They're usually **transparent**, but they cast reflections that cause them to resemble white- or cream-colored ovals.

In most cases, nits are difficult to detach from a host's hair, feathers, or skin. This is because female lice produce a sticky, waterproof substance when they lay their eggs. This substance cements the nits to their host organism. As a result, there is little chance the eggs will be shaken loose or rinsed away.

Nits stick to hair and must be combed out carefully to ensure removal.

Molting and Maturing

Nymphs, or baby lice, are ready to hatch after roughly one to two weeks. The newly hatched nymphs of human head lice are approximately the size of a pinhead. From their earliest moments, the babies of all species are completely independent and receive no care from their parents. Because they are born on or near a host organism, young lice usually start feeding right away.

Before reaching adulthood, a louse molts on three separate occasions. Molting is the process by which an animal sheds its exoskeleton. An exoskeleton is the rigid outer covering that provides invertebrates such as lice with protection and support. Between each molt, lice experience physical growth that eventually forces off their old exoskeleton. Once it has been shed, a new, larger shell is revealed. Following its third molt, a louse is considered mature. At this point, it is ready to reproduce.

A louse grows larger and larger each time it molts.

CHAPTER 4

Lice Past and Present

Scientists don't all agree on how or when lice **evolved**. One of the main reasons for this is a lack of louse **fossils**. Experts haven't found many remains of lice that date back to prehistoric times. They must therefore turn to other sources for clues about the history of lice. This often involves studying the fossils of prehistoric animals that may have served as host organisms.

Some scientists believe that members of the **order** Phthiraptera first appeared about 280 million years ago. In Greek, *phthir* means "lice," and the word *aptera* translates to "wingless." The first parasitic louse was probably related to book and bark lice, which feed on plant matter.

Experts suspect that chewing lice evolved earlier than sucking species. It's likely that they initially fed on the feathers and skin cells of birds. As time passed, the parasites began seeking out a wider variety of hosts. Eventually, certain species of lice started sucking their hosts' blood.

Fossils help scientists learn what the world was like millions of years ago and how different plants and animals have changed over time.

Four Separate Suborders

People continue to debate how to organize the different lice within the order Phthiraptera. Many scientists divide them into four **suborders**. These are Anoplura, Rhynchophthirina, Ischnocera, and Amblycera.

Members of Anoplura and Rhynchophthirina suck blood. The species within Anoplura feed off a broad range of mammals. They include human head and body lice. Meanwhile, only elephants and warthogs serve as hosts for the three Rhynchophthirina species.

Ischnocera and Amblycera are made up of chewing lice. Parasites within Ischnocera eat mainly the skin and feather cells of birds. This suborder contains the largest number of louse species. There are fewer members of Amblycera. Both birds and mammals act as host organisms for these lice.

Though there are thousands of species of Phthiraptera, most people are only familiar with those that affect humans. Head lice primarily impact children between 3 and 11 years old. Each year, they infest up to 12 million Americans in this age group.

Feather lice are members of Ischnocera.

Book and Bark Lice

Book and bark lice are more than the prehistoric ancestors of parasitic lice. These insects—which belong to the order Psocoptera—are also Phthiraptera's closest relatives. The lice in both orders share a similar body size and shape. Both orders also include species that use mandibles to chew food.

Unlike Phthiraptera, the species in Psocoptera are mostly free-living animals. In other words, they don't depend on host organisms to survive. They are able to obtain food from other sources.

Book lice eat **fungi** and mold. A bark louse's diet includes fungi as well, but it also features tree bark. Psocoptera lice are sometimes considered pests if they're found inside a person's home. For the most part, however, people tend to have far greater problems with Psocoptera's parasitic cousins.

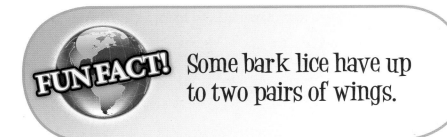

FUN FACT! Some bark lice have up to two pairs of wings.

A group of young bark lice swarm together on a leaf.

CHAPTER 5

People and Parasites

Very few lice species feed on human hosts. However, most people regard all lice as an unwelcome presence. In some cases, sucking lice spread diseases in **livestock** and pets. In other situations, chewing species cause animals to suffer from problems such as weight loss and skin irritation.

Human body lice are occasionally responsible for outbreaks of illnesses such as **typhus**. In contrast, human head lice do not spread disease. Nevertheless, both species are capable of causing discomfort. Some people are allergic to louse saliva. This is what triggers intense itchiness.

People who have lice frequently face fear and misunderstanding. It is common for friends and classmates to incorrectly assume that people suffering from lice have poor **hygiene**.

If you think you have a lice infestation, you should visit a doctor or nurse for a closer examination.

Increasing Public Awareness

Because they are fast-spreading pests, parasitic lice are animals that scientists want to learn more about. Public health officials are trying to increase awareness about preventing and treating lice infestations. For instance, some people don't know that human head lice are most commonly spread through head-to-head contact. A head louse doesn't normally travel across a bus, gym floor, or desks at school.

People may also not be aware that a person with head lice doesn't necessarily have poor hygiene. In fact, certain scientists believe these insects prefer clean hair. If people suspect they have head lice, it is best for them to be honest with parents, teachers, and medical workers. This makes it easier to manage an infestation.

Because lice are a part of nature and exist across the globe, it is important for people to understand how these parasites affect the world, and to learn how to cope with these pesky animals.

Scientists rely on microscopes and other equipment to get a closer look at lice.

Words to Know

abdomen (AB-duh-muhn) — the rear section of an insect's body

adaptations (ad-ap-TAY-shuhnz) — changes living things go through so they fit in better with their environment

bacteria (bak-TEER-ee-uh) — microscopic, single-celled living things that exist everywhere and that can be either useful or harmful

cells (SELZ) — the smallest units that make up living things

evolved (i-VAHLVD) — changed slowly and naturally over time

fossils (FOSS-uhlz) — bones, shells, or other traces of animals or plants from millions of years ago, preserved as rock

fungi (FUHN-gye) — plantlike organisms that have no leaves, flowers, roots, or chlorophyll and grow on plants or decaying matter

habitat (HAB-uh-tat) — the place where an animal or a plant is usually found

home remedies (HOME REM-i-deez) — nonprofessional treatments that often involve everyday household items used to cure health problems

hygiene (HYE-jeen) — keeping yourself and the things around you clean, in order to stay healthy

infestations (in-fes-TAY-shuhnz) — situations in which an environment or organism is invaded by unwanted life-forms

invertebrates (in-VUR-tuh-brits) — animals without a backbone

livestock (LIVE-stahk) sheep, horses, cows, pigs, or other animals that are kept or raised on a farm or ranch

mates (MAYTS) — animals that join together to reproduce

order (OR-duhr) — a group of related plants or animals that is bigger than a family but smaller than a class

parasites (PAR-uh-sites) — animals or plants that live on or inside of another animal or plant

pesticides (PES-ti-sides) — chemicals used to kill pests

predators (PREH-duh-turz) — animals that live by hunting other animals for food

reproduction (ree-pruh-DUHK-shuhn) — the act of producing offspring or individuals of the same kind

saliva (suh-LYE-vuh) — the watery fluid in your mouth that keeps it moist and helps you soften and swallow food

species (SPEE-sheez) — one of the groups into which animals and plants of the same genus are divided; members of the same species can mate and have offspring

suborders (SUB-or-durz) — groups of related life-forms classified within the same order

transparent (trans-PAIR-uhnt) — clear like glass and able to let light through so objects on the other side can be seen clearly

typhus (TY-fuss) — a disease that causes a purple rash, headaches, fever, and sometimes death

warm-blooded (WORM-BLUHD-id) — warm-blooded animals have a warm body temperature that does not change, even if the temperature around them is very hot or very cold

Habitat Map

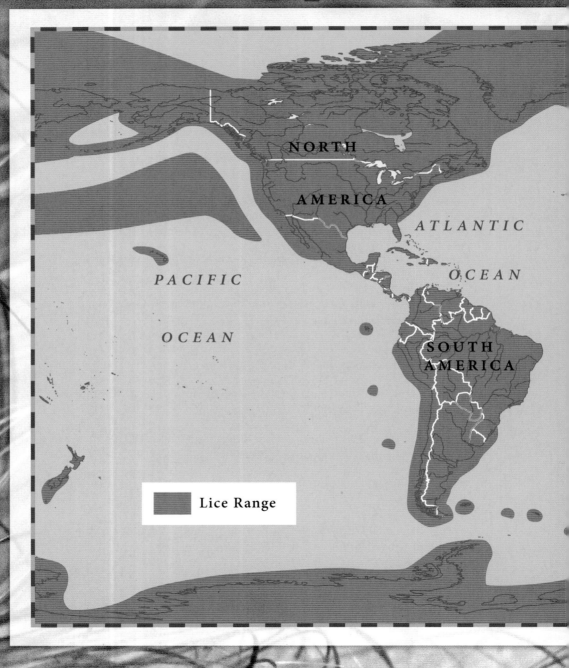

NORTH
AMERICA

ATLANTIC

OCEAN

PACIFIC

OCEAN

SOUTH
AMERICA

Lice Range

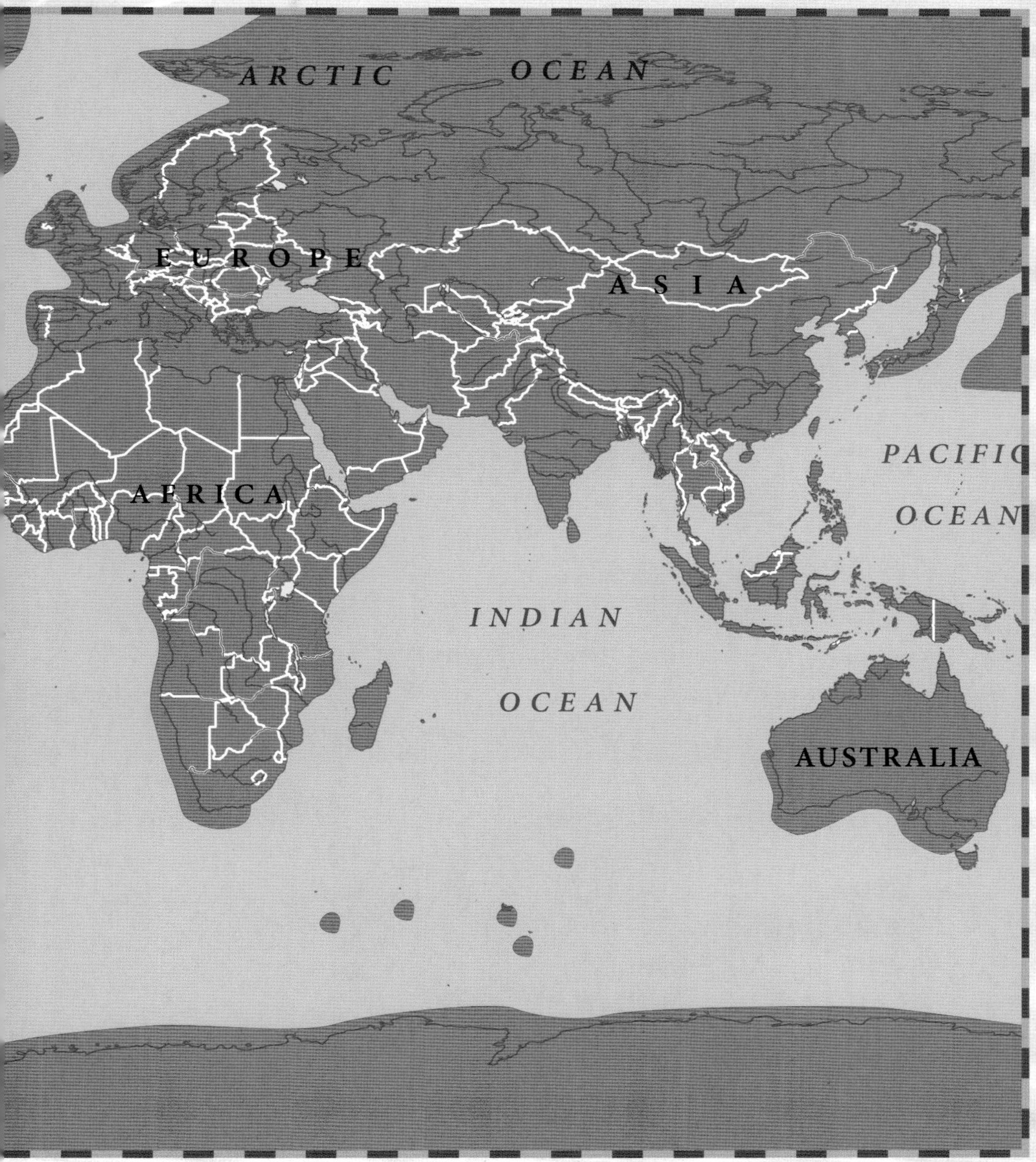

ARCTIC OCEAN

EUROPE

ASIA

AFRICA

PACIFIC OCEAN

INDIAN OCEAN

AUSTRALIA

Find Out More

Books

Gravel, Elise. *Head Lice*. Plattsburgh, NY: Tundra Books of Northern New York, 2015.

Kopp, Megan. *Parasites*. New York: AV2 by Weigl, 2012.

Visit this Scholastic Web site for more information on lice:
www.factsfornow.scholastic.com
Enter the keyword **Lice**

Index

Page numbers in *italics* indicate a photograph or map.

About the Author

Katie Marsico is the author of nearly 200 children's books. She learned a great deal while writing *Lice* and was surprised to find out about these insects' many remarkable adaptations. Still, Ms. Marsico hopes her knowledge of these parasites remains limited to books, interviews, and online research.